W9-DCB-516

The Countries

England

Pine Road Library
Lower Moreland Township
Huntingdon Valley, Pa.

Tamara L. Britton

ABDO Publishing Company

visit us at
www.abdopub.com

Published by ABDO Publishing Company, 4940 Viking Drive, Edina, Minnesota 55435.
Copyright © 2001 by Abdo Consulting Group, Inc. International copyrights reserved in
all countries. No part of this book may be reproduced in any form without written
permission from the publisher.

Printed in the United States of America, North Mankato, Minnesota.

Photos: Corbis
Editors: Bob Italia, Kate A. Furlong, and Christine Fournier
Art Direction & Maps: Neil Klinepier

Library of Congress Cataloging-in-Publication Data

Britton, Tamara L., 1963-
    England / Tamara L. Britton.
        p. cm. -- (The countries)
    Includes index.
    ISBN 1-57765-499-4
    1. England--Juvenile literature. [1. England.] I. Title. II. Series.

    DA27.5 .B755 2001
    942--dc21

                                                    00-052207

012001
032010

Contents

Hello!

Greetings from England! England is the largest country on the island of Great Britain. About 50 million people live there.

England has high mountains and low marshes. Many different plants and animals live there. It has a moderate climate.

England's government has a monarch. But a prime minister and Parliament govern the land. They make the laws to protect England's people.

The English people enjoy sports, music, and museums. They travel on modern trains and roads. And they make many products that support the **economy**.

England's past has been long. It has been influenced by many different **cultures**. Today, England is a strong country that is working to improve the lives of its people.

Hello from England!

Fast Facts

OFFICIAL NAME: England
CAPITAL: London

THE LAND
- Mountain Ranges: Pennine Mountains
- Highest Peak: Scafell Pike 3,210 feet (978 m)
- Major Rivers: Thames, Tweed, River Dee
- Largest Lake: Lake Windermere

THE PEOPLE
- Population: 50 million
- Major Cities: London, Birmingham
- Language: English
- Religion: Church of England (official), Catholic, Muslim, Hindu, Jewish

THE GOVERNMENT
- Form: Constitutional Monarchy
- Head of State: Monarch
- Head of Government: Prime Minister
- Flag: St. George's Cross
- Other Symbols: Union Jack
- Official Song: "God Save the Queen"
- Nationhood: 1066

THE ECONOMY
- Agricultural Products: Wheat, barley, corn, rye, potatoes, sugar beets, cows, sheep, poultry
- Mining products: Coal, oil, natural gas, sand, gravel, limestone
- Manufactured products: Processed foods, beverages, computers, cars, clothing, textiles, paper products
- Money: 1 pound sterling = 100 new pence

LONDON

English Pound Sterling

Timeline

700s B.C.	Celts move to England
A.D. 43	Romans begin ruling England
550s	Angles, Saxons, and Jutes conquer England
840	Vikings conquer England
1066	Normans conquer England
1642	Civil war begins
late 1700s	Industrial Revolution begins
1914-1918	World War I
1939-1945	World War II

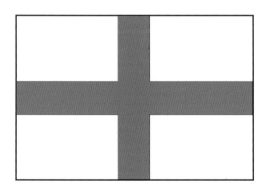

*England's flag is called
St. George's Cross.*

*The United Kingdom's flag
is called the Union Jack.*

Through the Ages

About 5,000 years ago, ancient people lived in England. They built stone monuments called henges. Then in about 700 B.C., Celts came to England.

In the following years, many groups tried to control England. Romans conquered it and ruled for nearly 400 years. Then **Germanic** tribes called Angles, Saxons, and Jutes took control. In 840, **Vikings** seized power. Then in 1066, Normans from France conquered England's land.

The Normans gave England a king. His name was William the Conqueror. After he died, a series of kings and queens continued to rule England for hundreds of years.

England's kings and queens greatly affected their country. Under King Edward I, England's Parliament began. King Henry VIII created a new church, called the Church of England. Under the rule of Queen Elizabeth I, England began building colonies in the New World.

Stonehenge is the most famous of England's ancient henges.

In 1642, King Charles I dismissed Parliament. This angered the people and led to a civil war. Then a citizen named Oliver Cromwell ruled England. After he died, kings and queens ruled England once again.

In the late 1700s, the Industrial Revolution began in England. It started when James Watt invented the steam engine. It allowed factories to produce more goods than ever before.

In 1914, England entered **World War I**. English troops traveled to France to help defeat the Germans. When the war ended in 1918, it had weakened England's empire.

Prime Minister Winston Churchill led England through **World War II**. It began in 1939. During the war, Germany bombed England and destroyed much of the country. But England and the **Allies** won the war in 1945.

In the following years, the English people rebuilt their country. Many English colonies gained independence. Today, England continues to be a strong presence in world affairs.

Winston Churchill (center) discusses battle plans during World War II.

England's Land

England is located on the island of Great Britain. It shares this island with Scotland and Wales. England occupies more than half of the island.

The waters in and around England are important. The Thames (tehmz) River is the longest river in England. A waterway called the English Channel separates England from France. Along England's coasts, there are harbors and **firths**. The coastal waters are also home to many beautiful islands.

Northern England has mountains. The Cumbrian Mountains contain Scafell Pike. At 3,210 feet (978 m), it is England's highest point. The Pennine Mountains divide northern England into eastern and western regions.

Northern England also contains the Lake District. It is a popular vacation spot. Lake Windermere, England's largest lake, is located there.

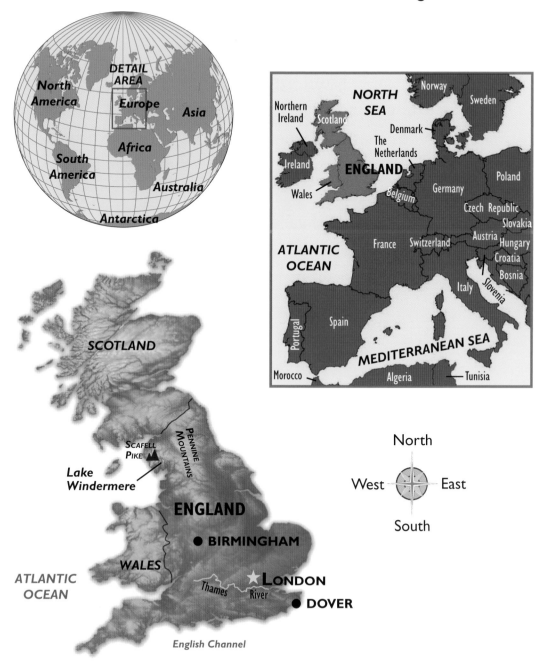

North America
DETAIL AREA
Europe
Asia
Africa
South America
Australia
Antarctica

NORTH SEA
Norway
Sweden
Northern Ireland
Scotland
Denmark
The Netherlands
Ireland
ENGLAND
Poland
Wales
Belgium
Germany
Czech Republic
Slovakia
ATLANTIC OCEAN
France
Switzerland
Austria
Hungary
Croatia
Bosnia
Slovenia
Italy
Portugal
Spain
MEDITERRANEAN SEA
Morocco
Algeria
Tunisia

SCOTLAND
PENNINE MOUNTAINS
SCAFELL PIKE
Lake Windermere
ENGLAND
BIRMINGHAM
WALES
ATLANTIC OCEAN
Thames River
LONDON
DOVER
English Channel

North
West
East
South

Central England has low **escarpments**. Along the central east coast is an area called the fens. It is a region of marshes that has been drained to make farmland.

Southern England has plains. It also has the North and South Downs. They are chalk hills. The hills surround an area of ridges and valleys called the Weald.

Many people think it rains a lot in England. But it only receives about 40 inches (120 cm) a year. The climate is moderate. It ranges from 35° F (2° C) to about 72° F (22° C). Sometimes, the temperature drops below zero. Northern England sometimes gets snow.

At Dover, the Downs lead to high, chalk cliffs called the White Cliffs of Dover.

Rainfall

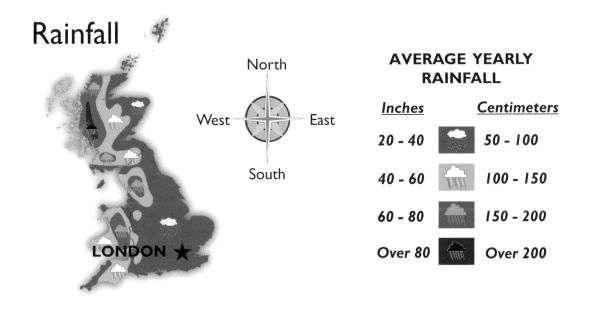

AVERAGE YEARLY RAINFALL

Inches		*Centimeters*
20 - 40		*50 - 100*
40 - 60		*100 - 150*
60 - 80		*150 - 200*
Over 80		*Over 200*

Temperature

Winter

Summer

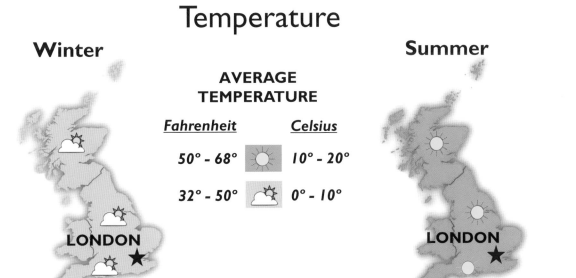

AVERAGE TEMPERATURE

Fahrenheit		*Celsius*
50° - 68°		*10° - 20°*
32° - 50°		*0° - 10°*

Plants & Animals

Hundreds of years of civilization have killed many of England's animals. Deer, rabbit, and wild horses live in England today. In London, foxes and hedgehogs are plentiful.

Forests cover less than ten percent of England's land. Much of the forests have been used up by years of industry. Overgrazing and draining marshes have also reduced England's forests.

Gardens in England contain most of the country's plants. Many gardens are well-kept and have existed for generations. The gardens are home to many birds. Bird watching has become a popular hobby in England.

A hedgehog

A garden in the English countryside

The English

England's long history has made it home to many people. Celts, Romans, and Anglo-Saxons were early settlers. Later, **emigrants** from England's colonies moved there. Today, England's people are a mix of all these **cultures**.

English people speak English. But some words are different from American English. In England, a television is called a telly, elevators are called lifts, and French fries are called chips. Some words are spelled differently, too. The word *color* is spelled *colour* and *favor* is spelled *favour*.

Many different religions are practiced in England. The Church of England is England's official church. People who belong to this church are called Anglicans. Most English people are Anglicans. Other English people may be Catholic, Muslim, Hindu, or Jewish.

English children come from many different backgrounds.

England has many types of homes. In the large cities, people often live in apartments, which are called flats. In the countryside, there are many cottages. The countryside also has large, historic estates with beautiful gardens.

Children in England must attend school until they are 16 years old. First, they go to primary school. Then they can go to grammar school or comprehensive school.

Some students then go to senior secondary school. To be admitted, they must pass the Common Entrance Examination. After completing senior secondary school, some students go to college.

England has many fine universities. Oxford and Cambridge are the most famous. Open University offers continuing education by **correspondence** and television.

Opposite page: Children practice reading at a school in London.

England's foods are as varied as its people. Asian dishes and spicy Indian curries now join traditional dishes, such as fish and chips. Breakfast, lunch, and dinner are the main meals. People also enjoy afternoon tea. It includes tarts, scones, jams, jellies, and of course, tea.

Visiting pubs is a popular activity in England. Pubs are places where people meet to relax with their friends and neighbors. While visiting a pub, people often order snacks and drinks.

Fish and chips consists of deep-fried fish and French fries. It is a popular and quick meal in England.

Raspberry Fool

I pound raspberries

sugar

I ounce butter

I pint heavy cream

Rinse and drain the raspberries and place them in a pan with the butter. Cook over low heat for about five minutes, mash slightly with the back of a spoon, then add sugar to taste. Let cool.

In a large bowl with an electric mixer, whip the cream. Fold the raspberries into the cream. Chill before serving. Serves 4.

AN IMPORTANT NOTE TO THE CHEF: Always have an adult help with the preparation and cooking of food. Never use kitchen utensils or appliances without adult permission and supervision.

American English	British English
Parking Lot _____	Car Park
Dessert _____	Pudding
Q-Tips _____	Cotton Buds
Drugstore _____	Chemist
Apartment _____	Flat
Vacation _____	Holiday
Uniform _____	Kit
Cookie _____	Biscuit

LANGUAGE

Products to Pounds

For many years, England's **economy** was based on farming. During the Industrial Revolution, many people worked in factories. Today, England's economy is based on many different industries.

More than half of English people work in service industries. They work in places such as banks, stores, and hotels.

Manufacturing also employs many English people. People process food and make chemicals. They make computers, cars, clothes, glass, and paper, too.

Tourism is another important industry in England. People from all over the world visit England's museums, gardens, and historic sites.

Some English people still work as farmers. They grow barley, corn, rye, potatoes, and sugar beets. Farmers also raise cows, sheep, and chickens.

Coal is the most important product mined in England. England has enough coal to supply the entire country. Oil, natural gas, and iron are also mined there.

Many English people work in service jobs, such as this travel agent.

Splendid Cities

London is England's capital and largest city. Romans founded it in the first century A.D. They called it Londinium. Today, more than 7 million people live there.

London has many famous landmarks. The Tower of London has served as a fortress, a royal palace, and a prison. Hyde Park, once a royal hunting ground, is now a place for visitors to relax. A clocktower called Big Ben watches over the city.

Central England is home to the city of Birmingham. It is England's second-largest city. It is also England's industrial center. Cars, bicycles, and motorcycles are made there. Engineering, metal trades, and service trades also contribute to its **economy**.

Opposite page: London is located along the banks of the Thames River.

England on the Go

People in England have many ways to get from place to place. In London, the famous red double-decker buses move people across the city. People in London can also ride on a subway called the Tube, or Underground.

Many people use cars to get around. In England, people drive on the left side of the road, not on the right side like U.S. drivers.

The Channel Tunnel, called the Chunnel, opened in 1994. It is a tunnel under the English Channel between England and France. The Chunnel has two, one-way tunnels that carry people and goods between the countries.

London's Heathrow International Airport is the busiest in England. More than 50 million passengers pass through it each year.

A double-decker bus carries passengers through London.

Governing England

England is part of the United Kingdom (U.K.). The U.K. includes England, Scotland, Wales, and Northern Ireland. These countries share a common government.

A monarch is the chief of state. He or she lives in Buckingham Palace in London. The monarch works with Parliament and the prime minister.

The prime minister is the head of the government. The prime minister is chosen because he or she is the head of the political party that holds the most seats in Parliament.

Parliament makes the laws for the government. It is made up of the House of Commons and the House of Lords.

England's monarch, Queen Elizabeth II, addresses Parliament.

All the countries in the U.K. have separate legal systems. In England, the Crown Court hears serious cases, such as murder. **Magistrates** hear less serious cases.

The houses of Parliament meet at Westminster Palace in London.

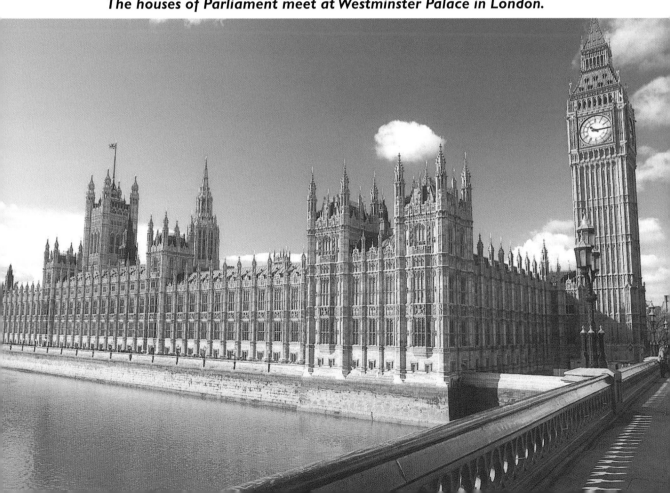

Celebrations

England's holidays are called Bank Holidays. Bank holidays include New Year's Day, Good Friday, Easter Monday, May Day, Guy Fawkes Day, Christmas Day, and Boxing Day.

May Day is celebrated on May 1. It marks the arrival of spring. A May Day queen is chosen to oversee each town's celebration. People listen to lively music and dance. Children weave ribbons around a maypole.

On November 5, people celebrate Guy Fawkes Day. Guy Fawkes tried to blow up Parliament in 1605. Today, people celebrate Guy Fawkes Day with bonfires and fireworks.

On December 25, people celebrate Christmas. They set up a Christmas tree and hang stockings. Father Christmas brings gifts to the children. The next day, people celebrate Boxing Day. They box gifts and give them to the poor.

These English children light sparklers to celebrate Guy Fawkes Day.

English Culture

England has a long tradition of rich **culture**. It has produced many famous writers, artists, and musicians. And English people have created new sports that are now played around the world.

Perhaps England's most famous writer is William Shakespeare. He wrote plays and **sonnets** during the late 1500s and early 1600s. Two of his most famous plays are *Hamlet* and *Romeo and Juliet*.

England's artists have also made great contributions to the world. Many of England's famous artists painted portraits. A well-known portrait is *Blue Boy* by Englishman Thomas Gainsborough.

William Shakespeare

Blue Boy *by Thomas Gainsborough*

English people listen to many kinds of music. Promenade Concerts feature classical music every year in London. English rock 'n' roll musicians such as the Beatles, the Rolling Stones, and Led Zeppelin have influenced many musicians around the world with their style.

Many English people enjoy sports. Soccer, which the English call football, is very popular. Tennis is another sport that many people enjoy. Two famous sports invented in England are cricket and rugby.

Cricket is played with a bat, a ball, and **wickets**. The batter hits the ball and then runs back and forth between two wickets as many times as possible.

In rugby, players carry or kick an oval-shaped ball. Fifteen people play on each team. Rugby is similar to American football.

Opposite page: A rugby match between England and Scotland

Glossary

Allies - countries that agree to help each other in times of need. During World War II, Great Britain, France, and the Soviet Union were called the Allies.

correspondence - classes given by mail or over the Internet rather than in a traditional classroom.

culture - the customs, arts, and tools of a nation or people at a certain time.

economy - the way a nation uses its money, goods, and natural resources.

emigrants - people who leave their country and move to another.

escarpment - a steep slope or cliff.

firth - a narrow inlet of sea that is located between cliffs.

Germanic - the people of northwestern Europe in the Middle Ages.

magistrate - a judge with the power to apply and enforce the law.

sonnet - a short, rhyming poem that is usually 14 lines long.

Vikings - daring seamen and warriors from northwestern Europe. Vikings raided the coasts of Europe in the 700s, 800s, and 900s.

wickets - two sets of stumps that are used in cricket. The ball is bowled at the wickets during the game.

World War I - 1914-1918, fought in Europe. The United States, England, France, and their allies were on one side. Germany, Austria-Hungary, and their allies were on the other side. The war began when Archduke Ferdinand of Austria was assassinated.

World War II - 1939-1945, fought in Europe, Asia, and Africa. The United States, France, England, the Soviet Union, and their allies were on one side. Germany, Italy, Japan, and their allies were on the other side. The war began when Germany invaded Poland.

Web Sites

The British Monarchy
http://www.royal.gov.uk/
This official Web site of the British monarchy answers questions about the monarchy, its history in England, and its role in today's government. This site also has official biographies and photographs of the royal family, including Queen Elizabeth II, Prince Charles, and Princess Diana.

English Heritage
http://www.english-heritage.org.uk/
The English Heritage Organization is responsible for preserving the country's historic buildings, landscapes, and monuments. Its site has information about famous landmarks in England and also has a special kids' section.

United Kingdom Virtual Journey
http://www.ontheline.org.uk/explore/journey/uk/ukindex.htm
This kid-friendly site has information about food, sports, art, and music in the United Kingdom. The Daily Life section allows visitors to follow the day of a ten-year-old English girl named Gwen.

These sites are subject to change. Go to your favorite search engine and type in "England" for more sites.

Pine Road Library
Lower Moreland Township
Huntingdon Valley, Pa.

Index